MANDALAS COLORING BOOK

Adult Coloring Books For Overcome Stress And Gain Relaxation

Mandala Craft Art

This book belongs to:

Color Swatch

Test your color supplies on this page to see how they react to the paper. Place a blank page or two behind each page as your color, to prevent bleed-through to the next page.

Color this mandala!

Color this mandala!

www.ingramcontent.com/pod-product-compliance
Lightning Source LLC
Chambersburg PA
CBHW081726250726
48657CB00010B/3151
* 9 7 8 1 7 0 2 2 8 6 5 8 9 *